THIS WALKER BOOK BELONGS TO:

_____

To Chris –
for the magical summer of rings
and wheels and circles
J.H.

To my brother John
M.C.

First published 1994 by Walker Books Ltd
87 Vauxhall Walk, London SE11 5HJ

This edition published 1996

2 4 6 8 10 9 7 5 3 1

Text © 1994 Judy Hindley
Illustrations © 1994 Margaret Chamberlain

This book was typeset in Bembo.

Printed in Hong Kong

British Library Cataloguing in Publication Data
A catalogue record for this book is available
from the British Library.

ISBN 0-7445-4730-X

WALKER BOOKS
AND SUBSIDIARIES
LONDON • BOSTON • SYDNEY

THE **WHEELING** AND **WHIRLING-AROUND** BOOK

Written by Judy Hindley

Illustrated by Margaret Chamberlain

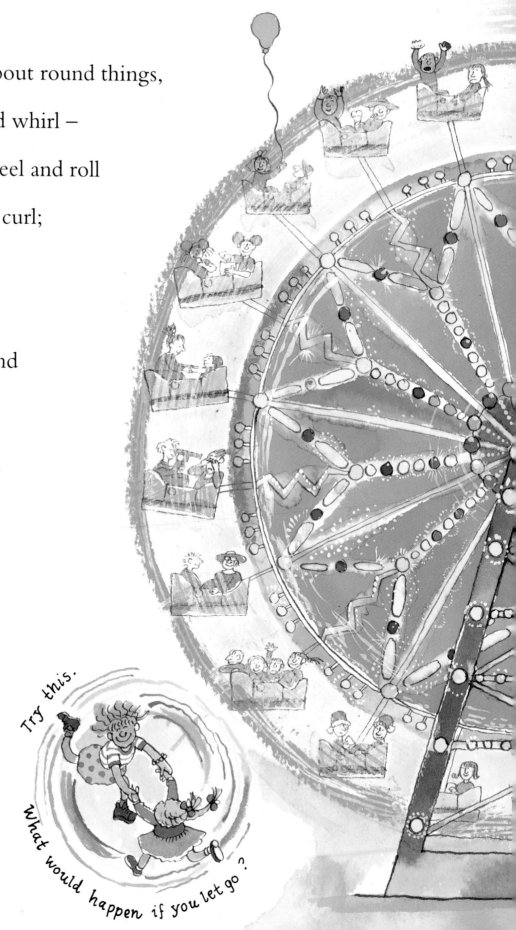

Let us think for a bit about round things,

and things that spin and whirl –

things that wheel and reel and roll

and curve and coil and curl;

things that are round

like a ball is round,

and things that are round

like a wheel,

and things that swing

in orbital rings,

out and about

and back again;

When something spins, two opposite things are happening at once: flying-apartness and holding-togetherness.

Try this. What would happen if you let go?

6

An orbit is the path of something travelling round something else.

and things you can

run your fingers round,

in a spiralling slope,

like an ice-cream cone;

and things you can hug,

like a tree.

Let us muse and gaze

and ponder,

and let our thoughts go free.

Let's give our eyes a wander,

and see what we can see!

Something dropped in the water makes it ripple into circles.

cone

cylinder

flat spiral

conical spiral

9

Every point on the rim of a circle is exactly the same distance from the centre.

Try this.
Draw a circle on paper and cut it out to make a paper disc. Now keep folding it in half... then open it out.

Do you see how all the folds meet in the centre?

A pizza is disc-shaped.

disc

WHERE'S MY HAT?

The imaginary line through a disc or sphere, round which it spins, is called its axis. Here's where the axis is on this disc.

A circular shape can do some things that other shapes can't do . . .

Let us begin

with things that spin

if you flip them along on the ground.

You can do it with coins and bottle tops,

you can do it with rings and crowns;

or dinner plates, or dustbin lids,

or the rim of your grandfather's hat…

You can race them or chase them or bowl them away

to be driven along by a breeze,

and they sometimes whizz quite a way, like that,

and go speeding along with ease,

till they finally falter and wibble and wobble and drop

on the side that's flat.

ghostly circle

ghostly arc

But what if you twirl

a thinnish disc

until it's a perfect blur?

You'll find what you've made

in a ghostly way

is the every-ways-round of a sphere —

12

ghostly sphere

ghostly ring

round like a pea

or a ping-pong ball,

or the eyes at the top of your face;

like marbles and cherries

and egg yolks and just about

everything orbiting way out in space!

13

Oh, a twirlable sphere is a great sort of shape,

but think what a terrible mess it can make!

Imagine a scatter of peas or pearls

or spherical sweets in a pack that's burst –

how perfectly ghastly to have in the street;

how disastrous to have on the stair!

For anything perfectly rollable

will be rolling to

everywhichwhere!

A sphere is the most common natural shape. Most huge things in the universe are spheres, like the billions of stars and planets in space.

Stars and planets are shaped into spheres by the holding-together force called gravity.

If you dumped all the water from a swimming-pool in space, it would become one vast water-drop. (Imagine diving in and out of it!)

Most of the tiniest natural things are spheres, like droplets and bubbles, and the eggs of zillions of small creatures.

Clinging and holding-togetherness makes droplets into spheres.

Rolling things about tends to make them round - like Plasticine rolled in the palms of your hands or pebbles rolled by the waves.

So STOP

and consider again your disc,

the spinnable thing you started with.

What's the name of the similar thing

on the things you know that go?

On bikes and trikes and trucks and cars

and roller-skates and apple-carts –

A solid disc makes a
very heavy wheel.
Joining the rim to
the hub with spokes
makes a wheel
much lighter –
so you can speed
it up and slow
it down more
easily.

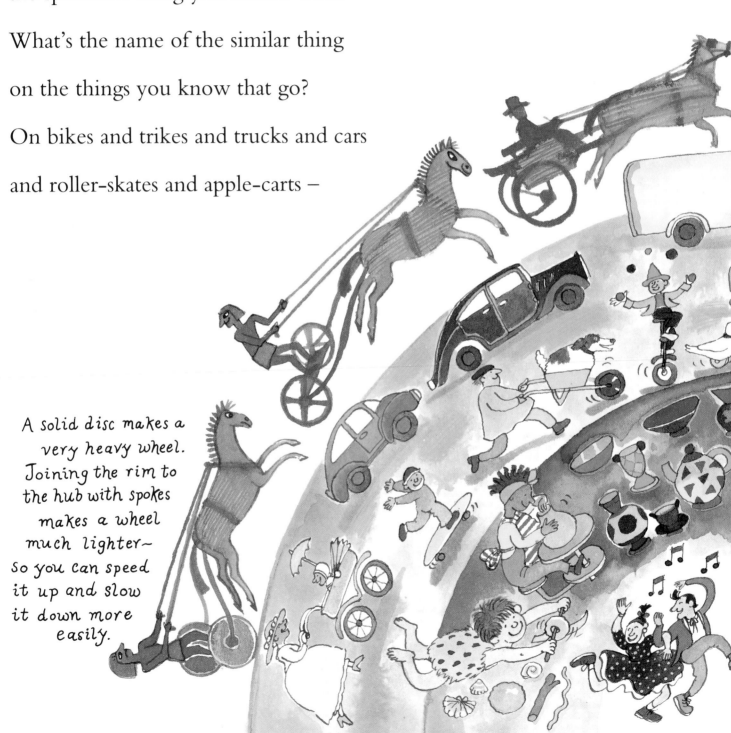

What shape is a knitting needle?

And spools

and tubes and

drums and pipes

and drinking straws,

and the crown of a hat?

And what about pistons

and rollers and rods

that make an engine go?

Now…

you can see you can make

a cylindrical shape

out of wheel upon wheel upon wheel.

But what if you sliced the skin of it off

in a curling, coiling peel?

21

can swoop us down, or whirl us up,

or carry us out and away –

can be flat as a spiral galaxy,

or the coil of a spider's web,

or go funnelling in

like a whirlwind

or water that glugs

from a tub.

No wonder

we yearn

to spin and turn

and go whirling

around

in rings –

from the tiniest atom

to weather and stars

there are so many

swirling

and orbiting

things…

Oh, let us dance

and sing!

It's not
surprising we
like to spin—like
everything else,
we're actually made of
invisibly tiny spinning
bits called atoms.

27

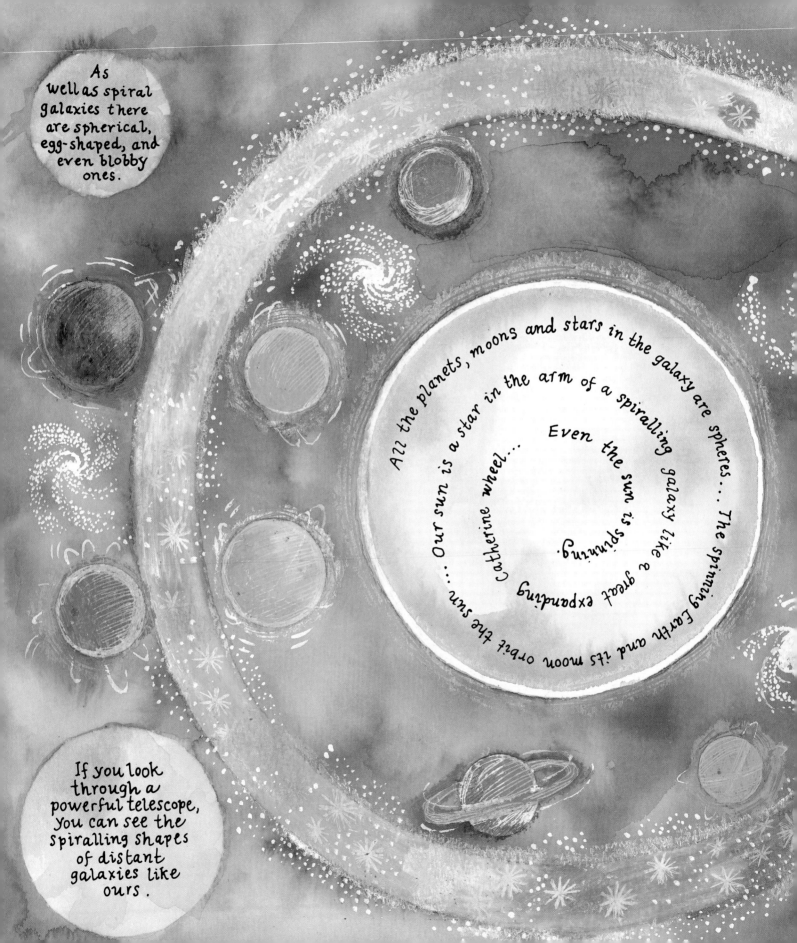

As well as spiral galaxies there are spherical, egg-shaped, and even blobby ones.

If you look through a powerful telescope, you can see the spiralling shapes of distant galaxies like ours.

All the planets, moons and stars in the galaxy are spheres... The spinning Earth and its moon orbit the sun ... Our sun is a star in the arm of a spiralling galaxy like a great expanding Catherine wheel... Even the sun is spinning.

The ball of the Earth spins like a top, turning day to night and day again.

Earth

a distant spiral galaxy

Oh, here we go

round the day again,

and here we go round the sun,

and here we go round the galaxy

in the curl of its glittering arm!

See how the giddiest games

we play,

and the tiniest things there are,

echo out

through the travelling universe,

unravelling star by star –

and it's all a part

of the dance of things,

the spinning-aroundness

and spiralling rings,

however small, however near,

however vast and far…

Index

Look up the pages to find
out about all these wheeling and
whirling-around things. Don't forget
to look at both kinds of words:
this kind *and* this kind .

MORE WALKER PAPERBACKS
For You to Enjoy

READ AND WONDER

An award-winning series of non-fiction picture books
full of facts and feelings about the real world.

"These books fulfil all the requirements of a factual picture book,
but also supply that imaginative element." *The Independent on Sunday*

"Beautifully illustrated books, written with style and humour."
The Times Educational Supplement

WHAT IS A WALL, AFTER ALL?
by Judy Allen/Alan Baron
0-7445-3640-5

THE WHEELING AND WHIRLING-AROUND BOOK
by Judy Hindley/Margaret Chamberlain
0-7445-4730-X

A PIECE OF STRING IS A WONDERFUL THING
by Judy Hindley/Margaret Chamberlain
0-7445-3637-5

A RUINED HOUSE
by Mick Manning
0-7445-4728-8

THINK OF AN EEL
by Karen Wallace/Mike Bostock

(Winner of the Times Educational Supplement Junior
Information Book Award and the Kurt Maschler Award)
0-7445-3639-1

ALL PIGS ARE BEAUTIFUL
by Dick-King Smith/Anita Jeram
0-7445-3635-9

£4.99 each

Walker Paperbacks are available from most booksellers, or by post from B.B.C.S., P.O. Box 941, Hull, North Humberside HU1 3YQ

24 hour telephone credit card line 01482 224626

To order, send: Title, author, ISBN number and price for each book ordered, your full name and address,
cheque or postal order payable to BBCS for the total amount and allow the following for postage and packing:
UK and BFPO: £1.00 for the first book, and 50p for each additional book to a maximum of £3.50.
Overseas and Eire: £2.00 for the first book, £1.00 for the second and 50p for each additional book.

Prices and availability are subject to change without notice.